What is the danger of reading Christian themes, morals and messages into the books we read, even if they are not present already?

_____
_____
_____
_____
_____
_____
_____
_____
_____
_____
_____
_____
_____
_____
_____
_____
_____
_____
_____
_____
_____
_____

How can we summarize what it means to "Apply a Christian Worldview" to our reading?

_____
_____
_____
_____
_____
_____
_____
_____
_____
_____
_____
_____
_____
_____
_____
_____

What is the final step of worldview analysis, after listening to and understanding the author?

_____
_____
_____
_____
_____
_____
_____
_____
_____
_____
_____
_____
_____
_____

If we are not to import Christian messages into the books we read, why should we even read them? Is it not dangerous to allow such opinions to go unchallenged?

_____
_____
_____
_____
_____
_____
_____
_____
_____
_____
_____
_____
_____
_____
_____
_____
_____
_____
_____
_____
_____
_____

What is the benefit of reading a nihilist author so as to understand nihilisim? Even granted that it is not dangerous, why is it desirable?

_____
_____
_____
_____
_____
_____
_____
_____
_____
_____
_____
_____
_____
_____
_____
_____
_____
_____
_____
_____
_____
_____
_____

In what sense do all great books tell "the truth?"

_____
_____
_____
_____
_____
_____
_____
_____
_____
_____
_____
_____
_____
_____
_____
_____
_____
_____

What about limits? Does the need for listening and understanding the author without reinterpreting him mean that ANY student should be exposed to ANY book, regardless of its content or intended audience?

_____
_____
_____
_____
_____
_____
_____
_____
_____
_____
_____
_____
_____
_____
_____
_____
_____
_____
_____

What is the appropriate age at which students should be exposed to literature from philosophical perspectives other than their own?

_____
_____
_____
_____
_____
_____
_____
_____
_____
_____
_____
_____
_____

PART 2

Your Equipment: The Socratic List

1) What does the story say about God?

    a. Does the world of the story include a God or higher power that governs events in some way? Is the higher power assumed to exist or is it mentioned explicitly?

    b. Who is God? Jehovah? Allah? Zeus? Fate? Chance? Nature?

    c. What is God like? Is he (or it) loving, judgmental, terrible, inscrutable, capricious, good, evil, --?

    d. What actions are ascribed to God in the story, either implicitly or explicitly?

    e. How does God relate to man? Is the relationship adversarial in some way? If so, who opposes whom?

    f. Do the story's answers to these questions tell the truth as THE AUTHOR saw it?

    g. Do the story's answers to these questions tell the truth as YOU see it?

2) What does the story say about human nature?

    a. What is a human being?

    b. Are human beings different from animals? In what ways?

    c. Are human beings created by some higher power, or is man his own god?

    d. Do human beings have souls? Eternal ones?

    e. Do human beings exist for a purpose? What is it?

    f. What adjectives might be used to describe human nature as it is presented in the story? Is it brave, generous, heroic, creative and benevolent? Is it frail, selfish, dull or evil?

    g. Do the story's answers to these questions tell the truth as THE AUTHOR saw it?

    h. Do the story's answers to these questions tell the truth as YOU see it?

3) What does the story say about the natural world?

    a. What rules govern the natural world in the story?

b. Is the natural world a source of good or evil in the story? What good things does it produce? What evil things?

c. Do the story's answers to these questions tell the truth as THE AUTHOR saw it?

d. Do the story's answers to these questions tell the truth as YOU see it?

4) What does the story say about human society and human relationships?

a. What rules govern human society and/or relationships in the story?

b. Are human relationships the source or occasion for good or evil in the story? What good things do they produce? What evil things?

c. Is human society the source or occasion for good or evil in the story? What good things does it produce? What evil things?

d. Do the story's answers to these questions tell the truth as THE AUTHOR saw it?

e. Do the story's answers to these questions tell the truth as YOU see it?

5) What is the highest good in the story?

a. How does the story measure or define success? Happiness? Value? Goodness?

b. What things does the story label good?

c. How does the story measure or define a good life?

d. Do the story's answers to these questions tell the truth as THE AUTHOR saw it?

e. Do the story's answers to these questions tell the truth as YOU see it?

6) What is the greatest evil in the story?

a. How does the story measure or define failure? Unhappiness? Futility? Evil?

b. What things does the story label evil?

c. Do the story's answers to these questions tell the truth as THE AUTHOR saw it?

d. Do the story's answers to these questions tell the truth as YOU see it?

7) In the world of the story, how can evil be overcome?

a. Are the story's characters powerless against the evil of the story?

b. Must they depend on outside help to overcome it? What sort of help?

c. Do the characters have to change in order to overcome evil? In what ways?

d. Do human relationships play a role in overcoming evil? What sort of role?

e. Do the story's answers to these questions tell the truth as THE AUTHOR saw it?

f. Do the story's answers to these questions tell the truth as YOU see it?

8) What does the story say about death?

a. Is there life after death? In what form?

b. Is death good or evil? Friend or foe?

c. Is death to be embraced or resisted? Why?

d. Is there such a thing as a good death? What would a good death look like?

e. Do the story's answers to these questions tell the truth as THE AUTHOR saw it?

f. Do the story's answers to these questions tell the truth as YOU see it?

9) What does the story say about love?

a. What behaviors in the story go by the name of love?

b. How does the story measure or define true love?

c. What power or significance does the story ascribe to love?

d. Do the story's answers to these questions tell the truth as THE AUTHOR saw it?

e. Do the story's answers to these questions tell the truth as YOU see it?

10) Who is the author?

a. What is the author's name?

b. Is the author a man or a woman?

c. How old was the author when he wrote the story?

d. Was the author happy or unhappy? Friendly or reclusive?

e. What kinds of relationships did the author have? Did he have a family? Was he an orphan?

f. Did the author suffer any hardships in his life that might have made him think or feel a certain way about his subject?

g. Do the answers to these questions influence in the author's story? In what ways?

11) Where did the author live?

a. In what country did the author live? In what city or state?

b. Did the author live in the city, or in the countryside?

c. Did the author live in poverty, or comfort?

d. Do the answers to these questions influence the author's story? In what ways?

12) When did the author live?

a. In what year was the author born? When did he die?

b. What events took place in the world during the author's lifetime? Did the author know about them? Was he involved in them?

c. Does the author refer to the events of his lifetime in his story?

d. Do the answers to these questions influence the author's story? In what ways?

13) What did the author believe?

a. Was the author a believer in a particular religion?

b. Was the author a member of a certain political party or other organization?

c. Was the author associated with a particular social cause or movement? (Examples include temperance, abolitionism, women's suffrage, civil rights, Puritanism, etc)

d. Was the author associated with a particular intellectual school or mode of literature? (examples include Romanticism, Transcendentalism, Existentialism, Naturalism, Realism, Postmodernism, etc)

e. Was the author's world view threatened by new philosophies, scientific discoveries or personal circumstances during his lifetime?

f. Did the author believe in a god? Which one?

g. Did the author believe that human life has purpose and meaning? If so, what did he believe that purpose or meaning to be?

h. What did the author believe to be the driving force that causes human events? Chance? Fate? Man's free will? God?

i. Do the answers to these questions influence the author's story? In what ways?

PART 3

Training Exercise:
"To Build a Fire" by Jack London

1.

Day had broken cold and gray, exceedingly cold and gray, when the man turned aside from the main Yukon trail and climbed the high earth-bank, where a dim and little-travelled trail led eastward through the fat spruce timberland. It was a steep bank, and he paused for breath at the top, excusing the act to himself by looking at his watch. It was nine o'clock. There was no sun nor hint of sun, though there was not a cloud in the sky. It was a clear day, and yet there seemed an intangible pall over the face of things, a subtle gloom that made the day dark, and that was due to the absence of sun. This fact did not worry the man. He was used to the lack of sun. It had been days since he had seen the sun, and he knew that a few more days must pass before that cheerful orb, due south, would just peep above the sky-line and dip immediately from view.

2.

The man flung a look back along the way he had come. The Yukon lay a mile wide and hidden under three feet of ice. On top of this ice were as many feet of snow. It was all pure white, rolling in gentle undulations where the ice-jams of the freeze-up had formed. North and south, as far as his eye could see, it was unbroken white, save for a dark hair-line that curved and twisted from around the spruce-covered island to the south, and that curved and twisted away into the north, where it disappeared behind another spruce-covered island. This dark hair-line was the trail—the main trail—that led south five hundred miles to the Chilcoot Pass, Dyea, and salt water; and that led north seventy miles to Dawson, and still on to the north a thousand miles to Nulato, and finally to St. Michael on Bering Sea, a thousand miles and half a thousand more.

3.

But all this—the mysterious, far-reaching hair-line trail, the absence of sun from the sky, the tremendous cold, and the strangeness and weirdness of it all—made no impression on the man. It was not because he was long used to it. He was a newcomer in the land, a chechaquo, and this was his first winter. The trouble with him was that he was without imagination. He was quick and alert in the things of life, but only in the things, and not in the significances. Fifty degrees below zero meant eighty-odd degrees of frost. Such fact impressed him as being cold and uncomfortable, and that was all. It did not lead him to meditate upon his frailty as a creature of temperature, and upon man's frailty in general, able only to live within certain narrow limits of heat and cold; and from there on it did not lead him to the conjectural field of immortality and man's place in the universe. Fifty degrees below zero stood for a bite of frost that hurt and that must be guarded against by the use of mittens, ear-flaps, warm moccasins, and thick socks. Fifty degrees below zero was to him just precisely fifty degrees below zero. That there should be anything more to it than that was a thought that never entered his head.

4.

As he turned to go on, he spat speculatively. There was a sharp, explosive crackle that startled him. He spat again. And again, in the air, before it could fall to the snow, the spittle crackled. He knew that at fifty below spittle crackled on the snow, but this spittle had crackled in the air. Undoubtedly it was colder than fifty below—how much colder he did not know. But the temperature did not matter. He was bound for the old claim on the left fork of Henderson Creek, where the boys were already. They had come over across the divide from the Indian Creek country, while he had come the roundabout way to take a look at the possibilities of getting out logs in the spring from the islands in the Yukon. He would be in to camp by six o'clock; a bit after dark, it was true, but the boys would be there, a fire would be going, and a hot supper would be ready. As for lunch, he pressed his hand against the protruding bundle under his jacket. It was also under his shirt, wrapped up in a handkerchief and lying against the naked skin. It was the only way to keep the biscuits from freezing. He smiled agreeably to himself as he thought of those biscuits, each cut open and sopped in bacon grease, and each enclosing a generous slice of fried bacon.

5.

He plunged in among the big spruce trees. The trail was faint. A foot of snow had fallen since the last sled had passed over, and he was glad he was without a sled, travelling light. In fact, he carried nothing but the lunch wrapped in the handkerchief. He was surprised, however, at the cold. It certainly was cold, he concluded, as he rubbed his numb nose and cheek-bones with his mittened hand. He was a warm-whiskered man, but the hair on his face did not protect the high cheek-bones and the eager nose that thrust itself aggressively into the frosty air.

6.

At the man's heels trotted a dog, a big native husky, the proper wolf-dog, gray-coated and without any visible or temperamental difference from its brother, the wild wolf. The animal was depressed by the tremendous cold. It knew that it was no time for travelling. Its instinct told it a truer tale than was told to the man by the man's judgment. In reality, it was not merely colder than fifty below zero; it was colder than sixty below, than seventy below. It was seventy-five below zero. Since the freezing-point is thirty-two above zero, it meant that one hundred and seven degrees of frost obtained. The dog did not know anything about thermometers. Possibly in its brain there was no sharp consciousness of a condition of very cold such as was in the man's brain. But the brute had its instinct. It experienced a vague but menacing apprehension that subdued it and made it slink along at the man's heels, and that made it question eagerly every unwonted movement of the man as if expecting him to go into camp or to seek shelter somewhere and build a fire. The dog had learned fire, and it wanted fire, or else to burrow under the snow and cuddle its warmth away from the air.

7.

The frozen moisture of its breathing had settled on its fur in a fine powder of frost, and especially were its jowls, muzzle, and eyelashes whitened by its crystalled breath. The man's red beard and mustache were likewise frosted, but more solidly, the deposit taking the form of ice and increasing with every warm, moist breath he exhaled. Also, the man was chewing tobacco, and the muzzle of ice held his lips so rigidly that he was unable to clear his chin when he expelled the juice. The result was that a crystal beard of the color and solidity of amber was increasing its length on his chin. If he fell down it would shatter itself, like glass, into brittle fragments. But he did not mind the appendage. It was the penalty all tobacco-chewers paid in that country, and he had been out before in two cold snaps. They had not been so cold as this, he knew, but by the spirit thermometer at Sixty Mile he knew they had been registered at fifty below and at fifty-five.

8.

He held on through the level stretch of woods for several miles, crossed a wide flat of niggerheads, and dropped down a bank to the frozen bed of a small stream. This was Henderson Creek, and he knew he was ten miles from the forks. He looked at his watch. It was ten o'clock. He was making four miles an hour, and he calculated that he would arrive at the forks at half-past twelve. He decided to celebrate that event by eating his lunch there.

9.

The dog dropped in again at his heels, with a tail drooping discouragement, as the man swung along the creek-bed. The furrow of the old sled-trail was plainly visible, but a dozen inches of snow covered the marks of the last runners. In a month no man had come up or down that silent creek. The man held steadily on. He was not much given to thinking, and just then particularly he had nothing to think about save that he would eat lunch at the forks and that at six o'clock he would be in camp with the boys. There was nobody to talk to; and, had there been, speech would have been impossible because of the ice-muzzle on his mouth. So he continued monotonously to chew tobacco and to increase the length of his amber beard.

10.

Once in a while the thought reiterated itself that it was very cold and that he had never experienced such cold. As he walked along he rubbed his cheek-bones and nose with the back of his mittened hand. He did this automatically, now and again changing hands. But rub as he would, the instant he stopped his cheek-bones went numb, and the following instant the end of his nose went numb. He was sure to frost his cheeks; he knew that, and experienced a pang of regret that he had not devised a nose-strap of the sort Bud wore in cold snaps. Such a strap passed across the cheeks, as well, and saved them. But it didn't matter much, after all. What were frosted cheeks? A bit painful, that was all; they were never serious.

11.

Empty as the man's mind was of thoughts, he was keenly observant, and he noticed the changes in the creek, the curves and bends and timber-jams, and always he sharply noted where he placed his feet. Once, coming around a bend, he shied abruptly, like a startled horse, curved away from the place where he had been walking, and retreated several paces back along the trail. The creek he knew was frozen clear to the bottom,—no creek could contain water in that arctic winter,—but he knew also that there were springs that bubbled out from the hillsides and ran along under the snow and on top the ice of the creek. He knew that the coldest snaps never froze these springs, and he knew likewise their danger. They were traps. They hid pools of water under the snow that might be three inches deep, or three feet. Sometimes a skin of ice half an inch thick covered them, and in turn was covered by the snow. Sometimes there were alternate layers of water and ice-skin, so that when one broke through he kept on breaking through for a while, sometimes wetting himself to the waist.

12.

That was why he had shied in such panic. He had felt the give under his feet and heard the crackle of a snow-hidden ice-skin. And to get his feet wet in such a temperature meant trouble and danger. At the very least it meant delay, for he would be forced to stop and build a fire, and under its protection to bare his feet while he dried his socks and moccasins. He stood and studied the creek-bed and its banks, and decided that the flow of water came from the right. He reflected awhile, rubbing his nose and cheeks, then skirted to the left, stepping gingerly and testing the footing for each step. Once clear of the danger, he took a fresh chew of tobacco and swung along at his four-mile gait.

13.

In the course of the next two hours he came upon several similar traps. Usually the snow above the hidden pools had a sunken, candied appearance that advertised the danger. Once again, however, he had a close call; and once, suspecting danger, he compelled the dog to go on in front. The dog did not want to go. It hung back until the man shoved it forward, and then it went quickly across the white, unbroken surface. Suddenly it broke through, floundered to one side, and got away to firmer footing. It had wet its forefeet and legs, and almost immediately the water that clung to it turned to ice. It made quick efforts to lick the ice off its legs, then dropped down in the snow and began to bite out the ice that had formed between the toes. This was a matter of instinct. To permit the ice to remain would mean sore feet. It did not know this. It merely obeyed the mysterious prompting that arose from the deep crypts of its being. But the man knew, having achieved a judgment on the subject, and he removed the mitten from his right hand and helped tear out the ice-particles. He did not expose his fingers more than a minute, and was astonished at the swift numbness that smote them. It certainly was cold. He pulled on the mitten hastily, and beat the hand savagely across his chest.

14.

At twelve o'clock the day was at its brightest. Yet the sun was too far south on its winter journey to clear the horizon. The bulge of the earth intervened between it and Henderson Creek, where the man walked under a clear sky at noon and cast no shadow. At half-past twelve, to the minute, he arrived at the forks of the creek. He was pleased at the speed he had made. If he kept it up, he would certainly be with the boys by six. He unbuttoned his jacket and shirt and drew forth his lunch. The action consumed no more than a quarter of a minute, yet in that brief moment the numbness laid hold of the exposed fingers. He did not put the mitten on, but, instead, struck the fingers a dozen sharp smashes against his leg. Then he sat down on a snow-covered log to eat. The sting that followed upon the striking of his fingers against his leg ceased so quickly that he was startled. He had had no chance to take a bite of biscuit. He struck the fingers repeatedly and returned them to the mitten, baring the other hand for the purpose of eating. He tried to take a mouthful, but the ice-muzzle prevented. He had forgotten to build a fire and thaw out. He chuckled at his foolishness, and as he chuckled he noted the numbness creeping into the exposed fingers. Also, he noted that the stinging which had first come to his toes when he sat down was already passing away. He wondered whether the toes were warm or numb. He moved them inside the moccasins and decided that they were numb.

15.

He pulled the mitten on hurriedly and stood up. He was a bit frightened. He stamped up and down until the stinging returned into the feet. It certainly was cold, was his thought. That man from Sulphur Creek had spoken the truth when telling how cold it sometimes got in the country. And he had laughed at him at the time! That showed one must not be too sure of things. There was no mistake about it, it was cold. He strode up and down, stamping his feet and threshing his arms, until reassured by the returning warmth. Then he got out matches and proceeded to make a fire. From the undergrowth, where high water of the previous spring had lodged a supply of seasoned twigs, he got his fire-wood. Working carefully from a small beginning, he soon had a roaring fire, over which he thawed the ice from his face and in the protection of which he ate his biscuits. For the moment the cold of space was outwitted. The dog took satisfaction in the fire, stretching out close enough for warmth and far enough away to escape being singed.

16.

When the man had finished, he filled his pipe and took his comfortable time over a smoke. Then he pulled on his mittens, settled the ear-flaps of his cap firmly about his ears, and took the creek trail up the left fork. The dog was disappointed and yearned back toward the fire. This man did not know cold. Possibly all the generations of his ancestry had been ignorant of cold, of real cold, of cold one hundred and seven degrees below freezing-point. But the dog knew; all its ancestry knew, and it had inherited the knowledge. And it knew that it was not good to walk abroad in such fearful cold. It was the time to lie snug in a hole in the snow and wait for a curtain of cloud to be drawn across the face of outer space whence this cold came. On the other hand, there was no keen intimacy between the dog and the man. The one was the toil-slave of the other, and the only caresses it had ever received were the caresses of the whip-lash and of harsh and menacing throat-sounds that threatened the whip-lash. So the dog made no effort to communicate its apprehension to the man. It was not concerned in the welfare of the man; it was for its own sake that it yearned back toward the fire. But the man whistled, and spoke to it with the sound of whip-lashes, and the dog swung in at the man's heels and followed after.

17.

The man took a chew of tobacco and proceeded to start a new amber beard. Also, his moist breath quickly powdered with white his mustache, eyebrows, and lashes. There did not seem to be so many springs on the left fork of the Henderson, and for half an hour the man saw no signs of any. And then it happened. At a place where there were no signs, where the soft, unbroken snow seemed to advertise solidity beneath, the man broke through. It was not deep. He wet himself halfway to the knees before he floundered out to the firm crust.

18.

He was angry, and cursed his luck aloud. He had hoped to get into camp with the boys at six o'clock, and this would delay him an hour, for he would have to build a fire and dry out his foot-gear. This was imperative at that low temperature—he knew that much; and he turned aside to the bank, which he climbed. On top, tangled in the underbrush about the trunks of several small spruce trees, was a high-water deposit of dry fire-wood—sticks and twigs, principally, but also larger portions of seasoned branches and fine, dry, last-year's grasses. He threw down several large pieces on top of the snow. This served for a foundation and prevented the young flame from drowning itself in the snow it otherwise would melt. The flame he got by touching a match to a small shred of birch-bark that he took from his pocket. This burned even more readily than paper. Placing it on the foundation, he fed the young flame with wisps of dry grass and with the tiniest dry twigs.

19.

He worked slowly and carefully, keenly aware of his danger. Gradually, as the flame grew stronger, he increased the size of the twigs with which he fed it. He squatted in the snow, pulling the twigs out from their entanglement in the brush and feeding directly to the flame. He knew there must be no failure. When it is seventy-five below zero, a man must not fail in his first attempt to build a fire—that is, if his feet are wet. If his feet are dry, and he fails, he can run along the trail for half a mile and restore his circulation. But the circulation of wet and freezing feet cannot be restored by running when it is seventy-five below. No matter how fast he runs, the wet feet will freeze the harder.

20.

All this the man knew. The old-timer on Sulphur Creek had told him about it the previous fall, and now he was appreciating the advice. Already all sensation had gone out of his feet. To build the fire he had been forced to remove his mittens, and the fingers had quickly gone numb. His pace of four miles an hour had kept his heart pumping blood to the surface of his body and to all the extremities. But the instant he stopped, the action of the pump eased down. The cold of space smote the unprotected tip of the planet, and he, being on that unprotected tip, received the full force of the blow. The blood of his body recoiled before it. The blood was alive, like the dog, and like the dog it wanted to hide away and cover itself up from the fearful cold. So long as he walked four miles an hour, he pumped that blood, willy-nilly, to the surface; but now it ebbed away and sank down into the recesses of his body. The extremities were the first to feel its absence. His wet feet froze the faster, and his exposed fingers numbed the faster, though they had not yet begun to freeze. Nose and cheeks were already freezing, while the skin of all his body chilled as it lost its blood.

21.

But he was safe. Toes and nose and cheeks would be only touched by the frost, for the fire was beginning to burn with strength. He was feeding it with twigs the size of his finger. In another minute he would be able to feed it with branches the size of his wrist, and then he could remove his wet foot-gear, and, while it dried, he could keep his naked feet warm by the fire, rubbing them at first, of course, with snow. The fire was a success. He was safe. He remembered the advice of the old-timer on Sulphur Creek, and smiled. The old-timer had been very serious in laying down the law that no man must travel alone in the Klondike after fifty below. Well, here he was; he had had the accident; he was alone; and he had saved himself. Those old-timers were rather womanish, some of them, he thought. All a man had to do was to keep his head, and he was all right. Any man who was a man could travel alone. But it was surprising, the rapidity with which his cheeks and nose were freezing. And he had not thought his fingers could go lifeless in so short a time. Lifeless they were, for he could scarcely make them move together to grip a twig, and they seemed remote from his body and from him. When he touched a twig, he had to look and see whether or not he had hold of it. The wires were pretty well down between him and his finger-ends.

22.

All of which counted for little. There was the fire, snapping and crackling and promising life with every dancing flame. He started to untie his moccasins. They were coated with ice; the thick German socks were like sheaths of iron halfway to the knees; and the moccasin strings were like rods of steel all twisted and knotted as by some conflagration. For a moment he tugged with his numb fingers, then, realizing the folly of it, he drew his sheath-knife.

23.

But before he could cut the strings, it happened. It was his own fault or, rather, his mistake. He should not have built the fire under the spruce tree. He should have built it in the open. But it had been easier to pull the twigs from the brush and drop them directly on the fire. Now the tree under which he had done this carried a weight of snow on its boughs. No wind had blown for weeks, and each bough was fully freighted. Each time he had pulled a twig he had communicated a slight agitation to the tree—an imperceptible agitation, so far as he was concerned, but an agitation sufficient to bring about the disaster. High up in the tree one bough capsized its load of snow. This fell on the boughs beneath, capsizing them. This process continued, spreading out and involving the whole tree. It grew like an avalanche, and it descended without warning upon the man and the fire, and the fire was blotted out! Where it had burned was a mantle of fresh and disordered snow.

24.

The man was shocked. It was as though he had just heard his own sentence of death. For a moment he sat and stared at the spot where the fire had been. Then he grew very calm. Perhaps the old-timer on Sulphur Creek was right. If he had only had a trail-mate he would have been in no danger now. The trail-mate could have built the fire. Well, it was up to him to build the fire over again, and this second time there must be no failure. Even if he succeeded, he would most likely lose some toes. His feet must be badly frozen by now, and there would be some time before the second fire was ready.

25.

Such were his thoughts, but he did not sit and think them. He was busy all the time they were passing through his mind. He made a new foundation for a fire, this time in the open, where no treacherous tree could blot it out. Next, he gathered dry grasses and tiny twigs from the high-water flotsam. He could not bring his fingers together to pull them out, but he was able to gather them by the handful. In this way he got many rotten twigs and bits of green moss that were undesirable, but it was the best he could do. He worked methodically, even collecting an armful of the larger branches to be used later when the fire gathered strength. And all the while the dog sat and watched him, a certain yearning wistfulness in its eyes, for it looked upon him as the fire-provider, and the fire was slow in coming.

26.

When all was ready, the man reached in his pocket for a second piece of birch-bark. He knew the bark was there, and, though he could not feel it with his fingers, he could hear its crisp rustling as he fumbled for it. Try as he would, he could not clutch hold of it. And all the time, in his consciousness, was the knowledge that each instant his feet were freezing. This thought tended to put him in a panic, but he fought against it and kept calm. He pulled on his mittens with his teeth, and threshed his arms back and forth, beating his hands with all his might against his sides. He did this sitting down, and he stood up to do it; and all the while the dog sat in the snow, its wolf-brush of a tail curled around warmly over its forefeet, its sharp wolf-ears pricked forward intently as it watched the man. And the man, as he beat and threshed with his arms and hands, felt a great surge of envy as he regarded the creature that was warm and secure in its natural covering.

27.

After a time he was aware of the first faraway signals of sensation in his beaten fingers. The faint tingling grew stronger till it evolved into a stinging ache that was excruciating, but which the man hailed with satisfaction. He stripped the mitten from his right hand and fetched forth the birch-bark. The exposed fingers were quickly going numb again. Next he brought out his bunch of sulphur matches. But the tremendous cold had already driven the life out of his fingers. In his effort to separate one match from the others, the whole bunch fell in the snow. He tried to pick it out of the snow, but failed. The dead fingers could neither touch nor clutch. He was very careful. He drove the thought of his freezing feet, and nose, and cheeks, out of his mind, devoting his whole soul to the matches. He watched, using the sense of vision in place of that of touch, and when he saw his fingers on each side the bunch, he closed them—that is, he willed to close them, for the wires were down, and the fingers did not obey. He pulled the mitten on the right hand, and beat it fiercely against his knee. Then, with both mittened hands, he scooped the bunch of matches, along with much snow, into his lap. Yet he was no better off.

28.

After some manipulation he managed to get the bunch between the heels of his mittened hands. In this fashion he carried it to his mouth. The ice crackled and snapped when by a violent effort he opened his mouth. He drew the lower jaw in, curled the upper lip out of the way, and scraped the bunch with his upper teeth in order to separate a match. He succeeded in getting one, which he dropped on his lap. He was no better off. He could not pick it up. Then he devised a way. He picked it up in his teeth and scratched it on his leg.

Twenty times he scratched before he succeeded in lighting it. As it flamed he held it with his teeth to the birch-bark. But the burning brimstone went up his nostrils and into his lungs, causing him to cough spasmodically. The match fell into the snow and went out.

29.

The old-timer on Sulphur Creek was right, he thought in the moment of controlled despair that ensued: after fifty below, a man should travel with a partner. He beat his hands, but failed in exciting any sensation. Suddenly he bared both hands, removing the mittens with his teeth. He caught the whole bunch between the heels of his hands. His arm-muscles not being frozen enabled him to press the hand-heels tightly against the matches. Then he scratched the bunch along his leg. It flared into flame, seventy sulphur matches at once! There was no wind to blow them out. He kept his head to one side to escape the strangling fumes, and held the blazing bunch to the birch-bark. As he so held it, he became aware of sensation in his hand. His flesh was burning. He could smell it. Deep down below the surface he could feel it. The sensation developed into pain that grew acute. And still he endured it, holding the flame of the matches clumsily to the bark that would not light readily because his own burning hands were in the way, absorbing most of the flame.

30.

At last, when he could endure no more, he jerked his hands apart. The blazing matches fell sizzling into the snow, but the birch-bark was alight. He began laying dry grasses and the tiniest twigs on the flame. He could not pick and choose, for he had to lift the fuel between the heels of his hands. Small pieces of rotten wood and green moss clung to the twigs, and he bit them off as well as he could with his teeth. He cherished the flame carefully and awkwardly. It meant life, and it must not perish. The withdrawal of blood from the surface of his body now made him begin to shiver, and he grew more awkward. A large piece of green moss fell squarely on the little fire. He tried to poke it out with his fingers, but his shivering frame made him poke too far, and he disrupted the nucleus of the little fire, the burning grasses and tiny twigs separating and scattering. He tried to poke them together again, but in spite of the tenseness of the effort, his shivering got away with him, and the twigs were hopelessly scattered. Each twig gushed a puff of smoke and went out. The fire-provider had failed. As he looked apathetically about him, his eyes chanced on the dog, sitting across the ruins of the fire from him, in the snow, making restless, hunching movements, slightly lifting one forefoot and then the other, shifting its weight back and forth on them with wistful eagerness.

31.

The sight of the dog put a wild idea into his head. He remembered the tale of the man, caught in a blizzard, who killed a steer and crawled inside the carcass, and so was saved. He would kill the dog and bury his hands in the warm body until the numbness went out of them. Then he could build another fire. He spoke to the dog, calling it to him; but in his voice was a strange note of fear that frightened the animal, who had never known the man to speak in such way before. Something was the matter, and its suspicious nature sensed danger—it knew not what danger, but somewhere, somehow, in its brain arose an apprehension of the man. It flattened its ears down at the sound of the man's voice, and its restless, hunching movements and the liftings and shiftings of its forefeet became more pronounced; but it would not come to the man. He got on his hands and knees and crawled toward the dog. This unusual posture again excited suspicion, and the animal sidled mincingly away.

32.

The man sat up in the snow for a moment and struggled for calmness. Then he pulled on his mittens, by means of his teeth, and got upon his feet. He glanced down at first in order to assure himself that he was really standing up, for the absence of sensation in his feet left him unrelated to the earth. His erect position in itself started to drive the webs of suspicion from the dog's mind; and when he spoke peremptorily, with the sound of whip-lashes in his voice, the dog rendered its customary allegiance and came to him. As it came within reaching distance, the man lost his control. His arms flashed out to the dog, and he experienced genuine surprise when he discovered that his hands could not clutch, that there was neither bend nor feeling in the fingers. He had forgotten for the moment that they were frozen and that they were freezing more and more. All this happened quickly, and before the animal could get away, he encircled its body with his arms. He sat down in the snow, and in this fashion held the dog, while it snarled and whined and struggled.

33.

But it was all he could do, hold its body encircled in his arms and sit there. He realized that he could not kill the dog. There was no way to do it. With his helpess hands he could neither draw nor hold his sheath-knife nor throttle the animal. He released it, and it plunged wildly away, with tail between its legs, and still snarling. It halted forty feet away and surveyed him curiously, with ears sharply pricked forward. The man looked down at his hands in order to locate them, and found them hanging on the ends of his arms. It struck him as curious that one should have to use his eyes in order to find out where his hands were. He began threshing his arms back and forth, beating the mittened hands against his sides. He did this for five minutes, violently, and his heart pumped enough blood up to the surface to put a stop to his shivering. But no sensation was aroused in the hands. He had an impression that they hung like weights on the ends of his arms, but when he tried to run the impression down, he could not find it.

34.

A certain fear of death, dull and oppressive, came to him. This fear quickly became poignant as he realized that it was no longer a mere matter of freezing his fingers and toes, or of losing his hands and feet, but that it was a matter of life and death with the chances against him. This threw him into a panic, and he turned and ran up the creek-bed along the old, dim trail. The dog joined in behind and kept up with him. He ran blindly, without intention, in fear such as he had never known in his life. Slowly, as he ploughed and floundered through the snow, he began to see things again,—the banks of the creek, the old timber-jams, the leafless aspens, and the sky. The running made him feel better. He did not shiver. Maybe, if he ran on, his feet would thaw out; and, anyway, if he ran far enough, he would reach camp and the boys. Without doubt he would lose some fingers and toes and some of his face; but the boys would take care of him, and save the rest of him when he got there. And at the same time there was another thought in his mind that said he would never get to the camp and the boys; that it was too many miles away, that the freezing had too great a start on him, and that he would soon be stiff and dead. This thought he kept in the background and refused to consider. Sometimes it pushed itself forward and demanded to be heard, but he thrust it back and strove to think of other things.

35.

It struck him as curious that he could run at all on feet so frozen that he could not feel them when they struck the earth and took the weight of his body. He seemed to himself to skim along above the surface, and to have no connection with the earth. Somewhere he had once seen a winged Mercury, and he wondered if Mercury felt as he felt when skimming over the earth.

36.

His theory of running until he reached camp and the boys had one flaw in it: he lacked the endurance. Several times he stumbled, and finally he tottered, crumpled up, and fell. When he tried to rise, he failed. He must sit and rest, he decided, and next time he would merely walk and keep on going. As he sat and regained his breath, he noted that he was feeling quite warm and comfortable. He was not shivering, and it even seemed that a warm glow had come to his chest and trunk. And yet, when he touched his nose or cheeks, there was no sensation. Running would not thaw them out. Nor would it thaw out his hands and feet. Then the thought came to him that the frozen portions of his body must be extending. He tried to keep this thought down, to forget it, to think of something else; he was aware of the panicky feeling that it caused, and he was afraid of the panic. But the thought asserted itself, and persisted, until it produced a vision of his body totally frozen. This was too much, and he made another wild run along the trail. Once he slowed down to a walk, but the thought of the freezing extending itself made him run again.

37.

And all the time the dog ran with him, at his heels. When he fell down a second time, it curled its tail over its forefeet and sat in front of him, facing him, curiously eager and intent. The warmth and security of the animal angered him, and he cursed it till it flattened down its ears appeasingly. This time the shivering came more quickly upon the man. He was losing in his battle with the frost. It was creeping into his body from all sides. The thought of it drove him on, but he ran no more than a hundred feet, when he staggered and pitched headlong. It was his last panic. When he had recovered his breath and control, he sat up and entertained in his mind the conception of meeting death with dignity. However, the conception did not come to him in such terms. His idea of it was that he had been making a fool of himself, running around like a chicken with its head cut off—such was the simile that occurred to him. Well, he was bound to freeze anyway, and he might as well take it decently. With this new-found peace of mind came the first glimmerings of drowsiness. A good idea, he thought, to sleep off to death. It was like taking an anaesthetic. Freezing was not so bad as people thought. There were lots worse ways to die.

38.

He pictured the boys finding his body next day. Suddenly he found himself with them, coming along the trail and looking for himself. And, still with them, he came around a turn in the trail and found himself lying in the snow. He did not belong with himself any more, for even then he was out of himself, standing with the boys and looking at himself in the snow. It certainly was cold, was his thought. When he got back to the States he could tell the folks what real cold was. He drifted on from this to a vision of the old-timer on Sulphur Creek. He could see him quite clearly, warm and comfortable, and smoking a pipe.

39.

"You were right, old hoss; you were right," the man mumbled to the old-timer of Sulphur Creek.

40.

Then the man drowsed off into what seemed to him the most comfortable and satisfying sleep he had ever known. The dog sat facing him and waiting. The brief day drew to a close in a long, slow twilight. There were no signs of a fire to be made, and, besides, never in the dog's experience had it known a man to sit like that in the snow and make no fire. As the twilight drew on, its eager yearning for the fire mastered it, and with a great lifting and shifting of forefeet, it whined softly, then flattened its ears down in anticipation of being chidden by the man. But the man remained silent. Later, the dog whined loudly. And still later it crept close to the man and caught the scent of death. This made the animal bristle and back away. A little longer it delayed, howling under the stars that leaped and danced and shone brightly in the cold sky. Then it turned and trotted up the trail in the direction of the camp it knew, where were the other food-providers and fire-providers.

Jack London's "To Build a Fire": Worldview Analysis

The questions and answers below present a discussion like the one found on the DVD recording, which is based on questions from the Socratic List. These are provided here along with their answers so that you can give your full attention to the oral discussion and begin to assimilate our discussion technique. In the next exercise, you'll be required to take your own notes!

Questions in this section are drawn from the Socratic List, which is found in Part 2 above. Answers are given in italics, and represent possible responses to the Socratic questions. You may, of course, answer the questions differently – these are provided as a guide to discussion only.

What does the story say about God?

Does the world of the story include a God or higher power that governs events in some way? Is the higher power assumed to exist or is it mentioned explicitly?

> *If there is a higher power in this story, it is the natural world. We might say that the natural world has endowed the dog and the man with instinct, and has endowed the man with intelligence as well.*

Who is God? Jehovah? Allah? Zeus? Fate? Chance? Nature?

> *Nature*

What is God like? Is he (or it) loving, judgmental, terrible, inscrutable, capricious, good or evil?

> *Nature is an impersonal force which operates by physical laws and chance.*

What actions are ascribed to God in the story, either implicitly or explicitly?

> *Nature kills the man, but selects the dog for survival.*

How does God relate to man? Is the relationship adversarial in some way? If so, who opposes whom?

> *Nature relates to man as an impersonal force, acting upon him relentlessly, exposing his weaknesses and eventually killing him.*

What does the story say about human nature?

What is a human being?

> *A certain kind of animal*

Are human beings different from animals? In what ways?

> *They are not really different from animals, except they have intelligence instead of just instinct, which may be seen as a hindrance rather than an asset. They are frail and unsuited to life in the natural world.*

Are human beings created by some higher power, or is man his own god?

There is no mention of God in this story and no reference to a higher power or to creation.

Do human beings have souls? Eternal ones?

There is no mention of souls or eternity in this story.

Do human beings exist for a purpose? What is it?

We can't detect a purpose for human existence in this story.

What adjectives might be used to describe human nature as it is presented in the story? Is it brave, generous, heroic, creative and benevolent? Is it frail, selfish, dull or evil?

Human nature is frail, dull and selfish, concerned only with survival.

What does the story say about the natural world?

What rules govern the natural world in the story?

The law of cause and effect governs the natural world, as demonstrated by the events that surround the man's death. Also, the law of instinct, which might be called the law of self-preservation, governs the relationship between the man and the dog. Finally, the law of chance has a significant role to play, as demonstrated by the circumstances that lead the man to build his fire beneath the snowy bough.

Is the natural world a source of good or evil in the story? What good things does it produce? What evil things?

The natural world is evil because it causes the death of the protagonist. On the other hand, the natural world is good because it provides the dog with instinct, the means of self-preservation.

What does the story say about human society and human relationships?

This story is not about human relationships. These were not the primary concern of the author, possibly because he did not see man as any different than an animal. The man is the only human being in the story.

What is the highest good in the story?

How does the story measure or define success? Happiness? Value? Goodness?

Survival is the best measure of success. Victory in the struggle for survival is the best gauge of happiness or value.

What things does the story label good?

Food, clothing, shelter and warmth.

How does the story measure or define a good life?

A life that is prolonged, even at the expense of someone else's.

What is the greatest evil in the story?

How does the story measure or define failure? Unhappiness? Futility? Evil?

Death is the greatest evil. Defeat in the struggle for survival is the measure of futility.

What things does the story label evil?

Hunger, cold, exposure.

In the world of the story, how can evil be overcome?

Evil is overcome by following instinct toward self-preservation, no matter where instinct leads.

Are the story's characters powerless against the evil of the story?

In a sense the man is powerless because of his lack of imagination, but more properly because of his lack of natural tools. He's not equipped to stave off death in this situation.

Do the characters have to change in order to overcome evil? In what ways?

In order to overcome death, the man would have to evolve into a higher life form. According to the doctrines of evolution, the man's death will eventually accomplish this for the whole species, but he cannot accomplish this change for himself.

What does the story say about death?

Is there life after death? In what form?

There is no hint in this story of a life after death. Death is the end.

Is death good or evil? Friend or foe?

Aside from "culling the herd" of unfit individuals, which evolutionary theory would call a good function, death is a great evil, the ultimate evil, the embodiment of all that is evil.

Is death to be embraced or resisted? Why?

It is to be avoided and staved off at all costs, even that of killing others in order to survive.

Is there such a thing as a good death? What would a good death look like?

No, death is the end, the enemy. There is no good death.

What does the story say about love?

Love, a uniquely human emotion separate from that of animals, is not represented in this story.

When did the author live?

In what year was the author born? When did he die?

1876-1916

What events took place in the world during the author's lifetime? Did the author know about them? Was he involved in them?

London journeyed to the Yukon Territory in 1897 along with countless others hoping to make a score in the gold rush. In November 1897, he staked a claim in Henderson Creek, the destination of the man in "To Build a Fire." Though he left Alaska the following summer without much gold, he would draw from his rich experiences in the northern wilds for many of his lasting works, including Call of the Wild and White Fang and, of course, 1908's "To Build a Fire," usually considered his most lasting work.

What did the author believe?

Was the author a believer in a particular religion?

No

Was the author a member of a certain political party or other organization?

London was an ardent socialist

Was the author associated with a particular intellectual school or mode of literature? (Examples include Romanticism, Transcendentalism, Existentialism, Naturalism, Realism, Postmodernism, etc)

Jack London is usually considered a literary Naturalist, along with authors such as Stephen Crane (Red Badge of Courage) and Theodore Dreiser (Sister Carrie).

Naturalistic writers were influenced by the evolution theory of Charles Darwin who, in his monumental 1859 work On the Origin of Species, theorized that environments alter the biology and behavior of organisms; the organisms whose traits promote survival reproduce more successfully and adapt new, more efficient traits. (Survival of the fittest)

Naturalists saw the world through evolutionary eyes and concluded that it was deterministic – that is, that it proceeded by a series of physical cause-and-effect relationships. Human actions, even, have been caused by prior environmental, social, and biological factors beyond the control of the individual.

Naturalistic works exposed the dark harshness of life, including poverty, racism, prejudice, disease, prostitution, filth, etc. They were often very pessimistic and frequently criticized for being too blunt. In the United States, the genre is associated principally with writers such as Stephen Crane, Frank Norris, and Theodore Dreiser.

This deterministic view of life common to naturalists influenced their writing in a number of areas. Since humans do not have free will, the naturalists often refrained from making moral judgments on the actions of their characters; after all, the environment, and not the human, has determined these actions.

The naturalists also viewed the deterministic environment as indifferent and harsh to its inhabitants; accordingly, keen instinct rather than civilized intellect is necessary for survival (in "To Build a Fire," for example, the man is lacking this instinct).

What did the author believe to be the driving force that causes human events? Chance? Fate? Man's free will? God?

London was an evolutionist and so believed that physical cause and effect, guided by chance, was the driving force behind human events.

*****

Not a Sermon

As is clear from the foregoing analysis, Jack London's story advocates many ideas that flatly contradict the principles of Christianity. Nevertheless, the story gives us a wonderful opportunity to talk about the real truth of God's world – all without using any Christian lingo. The book is, after all, no sermon. Any attempt to make it a sermon involves a process that is antithetical to good reading. As C.S. Lewis says in his *Experiment in Criticism,*

> *"[Appreciation of literature] demands the opposite process. We must not make books the vehicles of our own subjectivity. We must begin by laying aside as completely as we can all our own preconceptions, interests and associations. Then, we must use our eyes. We must look, and go on looking until we have seen exactly what is there. We sit down before the picture in order to have something done to us, not that we may do things with it. The first demand any work of art makes upon us is surrender. Look. Listen. Receive. Get yourself out of the way. There is no good asking first whether work before you deserves such a surrender, for until you have surrendered you cannot possibly find out."*

In literature, this receiving involves asking and answering the basic question: "what does the author say?" Figure this out, and you are doing the real work of literary analysis.

Sometimes, however, the author's message is one of despair, discouragement, defeat. Though it certainly is no sermon, you may feel the need for a sermon after reading it! Likewise, our students sometimes need reminding of the truth of the Gospel after confronting the well articulated views of a non-believer. These stories give us the chance to confront them with darkness and remind them of the light in the same lesson.

We must remember, however, not to give them the sermon beforehand! They must read the work for what it is, see it in all its fullness before they go interpreting. And this for their own good, for unless they see the pessimism of all other worldviews and see how bleak they really are, they have no need of the Gospel. The Gospel is described as a great light coming into a world of darkness. One role of classic literature is to demonstrate the darkness so our students see their need for light.

PART 4

Training Exercise:
Flannery O'Connor's "Revelation"

Flannery O'Connor's stories are not in the public domain; it is therefore not possible to include the full text of "Revelation" in this syllabus.

The book is still in print, however, and is available in a variety of formats.

"Revelation" first appeared in Flannery O'Connor's final short story collection *Everything that Rises Must Converge,* which was published in 1965, two years after the author's death.

Everything That Rises Must Converge

Paperback: 320 pages

Publisher: Farrar, Straus and Giroux (1965)

ISBN-10: 0374504644

ISBN-13: 978-0374504649

You can buy an e-book or a print copy directly from the publisher at

http://us.macmillan.com/books/9781466829039.

The publisher also gives you the option of purchasing from various other retailers through the website.

Though we only discuss "Revelation" in this presentation, we also highly recommend O'Connor's other stories for their stark portrayal of man's need for grace and the strange guises it often wears when barging in to rescue him.

Flannery O'Connor's "Revelation": Worldview Analysis

In this exercise, written answers have been reomved, leaving only the discussion questions themselves. Use the space provided after each question to take notes from the DVD discussion in addition to jotting down your own reactions, comments and ideas.

Questions from the *Teaching the Classics* basic seminar (designed to reveal the structure and main themes of the story):

Who is the protagonist in this story? Who is the Antagonist?

_____
_____
_____
_____
_____
_____
_____
_____
_____
_____

What types of conflict drive this story forward?

_____
_____
_____
_____
_____
_____
_____
_____
_____
_____

Is the conflict a man v. himself struggle?

_____
_____
_____
_____
_____
_____
_____
_____

Is the conflict a man v. man struggle?

_____
_____
_____
_____
_____
_____
_____
_____
_____

When and where does this story take place?

_____
_____
_____
_____
_____
_____
_____
_____
_____

What events form the climax of this story?

_____
_____
_____
_____
_____
_____
_____
_____
_____

What does the main character learn in this story?

_____
_____
_____
_____

Questions from the Socratic List for Worldview Analysis (found in Part 2 of this syllabus):

1. What does the story say about God?

_____

_____

_____

_____

_____

_____

_____

_____

_____

_____

_____

_____

_____

_____

_____

_____

_____

_____

_____

2. What does the story say about human nature?

_____

_____

_____

_____

_____

_____

_____

_____

_____

_____

_____

_____

_____

_____

2b. Are human beings different from animals? In what ways?

_____
_____
_____
_____
_____
_____
_____
_____
_____
_____
_____
_____
_____
_____
_____
_____
_____
_____
_____

2f. What adjectives might be used to describe human nature as it is presented in the story? Is it brave, generous, heroic, creative and benevolent? Is it frail, selfish, dull or evil?

_____
_____
_____
_____
_____
_____
_____
_____
_____
_____
_____
_____
_____
_____
_____
_____
_____
_____
_____

3. What does the story say about the natural world?

_____
_____
_____
_____
_____
_____
_____
_____
_____
_____
_____
_____
_____
_____
_____
_____
_____
_____

4. What does the story say about human society and human relationships?

_____
_____
_____
_____
_____
_____
_____
_____
_____
_____
_____
_____
_____
_____
_____
_____
_____

6. What is the greatest evil in the story?

_____
_____
_____
_____
_____
_____
_____
_____
_____
_____
_____
_____
_____
_____
_____
_____
_____

7. In the world of the story, how can evil be overcome?

_____
_____
_____
_____
_____
_____
_____
_____
_____
_____
_____
_____
_____
_____
_____
_____

5. What is the highest good in the story?

_____

_____

_____

_____

_____

_____

_____

_____

_____

_____

_____

_____

_____

_____

_____

_____

5c. How does the story measure or define a good life?

_____

_____

_____

_____

_____

_____

_____

_____

_____

_____

_____

_____

_____

_____

_____

_____

Do the story's answers to these questions tell the truth?

_____
_____
_____
_____
_____
_____
_____
_____
_____
_____
_____
_____
_____
_____
_____
_____
_____
_____
_____
_____
_____
_____
_____
_____
_____
_____
_____
_____
_____
_____
_____
_____
_____
_____
_____
_____
_____

APPENDIX A

Major Periods in English Language Literature

Worldview analysis of a work of literature begins with an understanding of the work's context. This invariably requires some knowledge of the period in which the work was written, and what ideas or movements influenced its composition. This appendix provides an overview of the history of English language literature.

Major Periods in English Language Literature

In the broadest terms, English language literature has undergone six major periods or movements since ancient times. They are usually described as follows (with very rough dates in parentheses):

- **Medieval** (500 – 1500 A.D.), beginning with the fall of Rome and continuing until the Renaissance;

- **Renaissance** (1500 – 1660), ending with the Restoration of Charles II;

- **Neo-classical** (1660 – 1800), beginning with the Restoration and continuing through the end of the revolutionary period, when it was known as the "Age of Enlightenment";

- **Romantic** (1800 – 1865), beginning in the last decades of the 18th century and continuing through the middle of the 19th;

- **Realist** (1840 – 1914), beginning in England with the accession of Queen Victoria and in America after the Civil War, and continuing up to WWI; and

- **Modern** (1900 – 1945), running from the turn of the twentieth century to the end of WWII.

Each of these labels reflects a system of broad assumptions about the world that was more or less generally accepted by thinkers of the period. Familiarity with these assumptions can help you place the books you read in the proper historical and philosophical context – a key first step in worldview analysis. If you know what characteristics generally apply to works of Realism, for example, you'll have a clue about Mark Twain's attitude toward his subject even before you read *Huckleberry Finn*.

Two Important Cautions

Thinking in terms of literary periods is a powerful way to understand an author's world view. However, it is not as simple as it sounds at first. Two main cautions are necessary:

Sub-periods

Within each literary period, there are variations that allow for the identification of distinct movements. *Elizabethan*, for example, is a special category of late *Renaissance* literature that includes William Shakespeare but excludes Thomas More, while the label *Victorian* corresponds to a particular kind of 19th century English *Realism* that includes Charles Dickens but not Mark Twain. It is helpful to remember that categorizing something is itself a work of interpretation, and there are as many ways to do it as there are interpreters. This guide will stick to the broadest and most generally agreed upon labels.

Overlap

New literary periods don't begin and end all at once, of course. Assumptions and conventions change gradually and unevenly, depending upon time, place and personality. The governing ideas of one period often linger long into the next, informing and shaping its development. This means that it is sometimes difficult to assign definitive dates to a particular period. For example, we can date the beginning of the Victorian period very specifically: 1837, when Victoria rose to the throne of England. It is more difficult to say exactly when Realism became the dominant mode of English literature.

Also, the fact that an author lived in a particular period doesn't necessarily mean his work bows to the conventions of that period. Literary history is full of examples of authors whose work foreshadowed future developments, or hearkened back to days gone by. Emily Bronte's *Wuthering Heights*, for example, though written in the Victorian period, has much in common with works of the Romantic period which came before. By the same token, the works of Jane Austen seem to foreshadow the Victorian age, even though they were written during the height of Romanticism.

In the end, it is best to use your understanding of literary periods as a collection of "hints" about the world view assumptions of great authors. It can be a great way quickly to explain the differences between Jack London and Nathaniel Hawthorne, for example, and pave the way for deeper study of their individual careers.

Sources

Reference texts such as the Norton Anthologies are excellent sources for information on literary periods and worldviews. In addition, they contain sizable excerpts from important works in each period. In many cases, texts are included in their entirety. In our view these volumes are worth owning as they provide an invaluable survey of Western literature.

The Norton Anthology of English Literature, 5th ed. (New York: Norton, 1986)

The Norton Anthology of American Literature, 2nd ed. (New York: Norton, 1985)

How To Use This Appendix:

This appendix is designed to prepare you for world view analysis by providing a summary of assumptions and themes common to literary works from each of the periods mentioned above. In addition, we have created a list of notable authors from each period and some of their most important works. Please note that the lists are not intended to be exhaustive. Authors and works have been included in order to illustrate and provide examples of the worldviews in question. For this reason, too, we have included some works of poetry and philosophy as well as fiction.

Finally, we have provided space for you to add to this list as you discover other titles that help you present worldview issues in your own classroom.

As with all lists, it is necessary to understand the purpose of this appendix before you dive in and begin assigning books. Some booklists are created for the purpose of saying, "Here's a list of books that are good for you. You can feel perfectly safe assigning any of these books to your student, regardless of his age or experience."

This is **not** that kind of list.

The titles on this list have been chosen because they represent (to one degree or another) major worldview trends in Western thought. They are included because they will provide your students with the opportunity to engage with worldviews other than their own. You may find the content of some of these titles disturbing or offensive – in many cases, their first readers felt the same way.

This is especially true of the modernist period, which arose because authors felt disconnected from traditional morality and traditional world views. As a result, you will find little support for traditional morality in modernist literature! Do not expect to find it – do not be surprised if you find the opposite instead. If you are looking to Ernest Hemingway to encourage and support your students in a Christian way of thinking, you are looking in the wrong place.

If, however, your student is ready to try his hand at interpretation of the world's most influential literature and to practice taking every thought captive to the obedience of Christ, the books in this appendix are just what you need!

I. Medieval Literature (500-1500)

Anglo-Saxon (500-1066)

The term "Anglo-Saxon" applies to literature produced between the invasion of Celtic England by Germanic tribes in the fifth century and the conquest of England in 1066 by William the Conqueror. This literature is heavily based on the tradition of oral storytelling, and includes epic poems such as *Beowulf*. Thematically, Anglo-Saxon literature often addressed the *heroic ideal*, which was a picture of kingly behavior that reflected the basic political and social relationship of Anglo-Saxon society: the bond between a king and his warriors. The heroic ideal involved responsibility, leadership, loyalty, generosity and, above all, skill in battle. Anglo-Saxon literature existed in part to praise the heroic virtues of its kings and so secure their eternal fame.

Anglo-Saxon England was Christianized in the 7th century, and from that date its literature became overwhelmingly Christian in its subject matter. Interestingly enough, however, it still retained its concern for the heroic ideal, and the result was a mingling of Christian and pagan elements. Biblical figures like Moses, Jesus and even God the Father often appeared as Beowulf-like heroes, performing mighty deeds.

Authors: Anglo-Saxon Literature

Anonymous
The Dream of the Rood (seventh century)
Beowulf (eighth century)
The Battle of Maldon (tenth century)

Caedmon
Hymn (seventh century)

Middle English (1066 -1500)

The Norman conquest of England in 1066 marks a significant change in the development of English literature. Where Anglo-Saxon literature had been written by and for the aristocracy (that is, kings and their households), Middle English literature was popular literature, written by and for people of the lower classes.

This change had a significant effect on the subject matter of Middle English literature. Its heroes, for example, were not the idealized kings of the Anglo-Saxon period; instead, they were real human protagonists who not only fought but also laughed, cried, played games, and above all, fell in and out of love. The situations of ordinary life played a much larger part in Middle English literature than they had before 1066.

Despite its new directions, Middle English literature continued to reflect the centrality of Christianity in the medieval world. Virtually all works, whether sacred or secular, dealt with issues such as personal salvation and the institutional church. Even the courtly love tales which were popular throughout the medieval period were told from within the framework of Christian doctrines such as sin, self-sacrifice and piety.

Authors: Middle English Literature

Anonymous
Piers Plowman (c. 1372-1389)
Sir Gawain and the Green Knight (c. 1375-1400)
Everyman (after 1485)

Geoffrey Chaucer (c. 1343-1400)
The Canterbury Tales (c. 1386-1400)

Margery Kempe (1373-1438)
The Book of Margery Kempe (date unknown)

Sir Thomas Malory (c. 1405-1471)
Morte Darthur (1485)

Other Works of Medieval Literature:

_____

_____

_____

_____

_____

_____

_____

_____

_____

_____

_____

II. Renaissance Literature (1500-1660)

The English Renaissance is usually dated from the accession of Henry Tudor in 1485. The literature of this period was affected by several very different movements, from Renaissance humanism and the Protestant Reformation to English nationalism, which came of age under Queen Elizabeth I (r. 1558-1603). It is notoriously difficult to define a "Renaissance worldview," but the career of Sir Philip Sydney is perhaps the best illustration. Sydney was a courtier to Elizabeth I and served her as a foreign ambassador; he was a patron of the arts and a humanist scholar in his own right; he was a poet whose Petrarchan sonnets rank among the finest in history; he was the greatest literary critic of his day; he was an earnest supporter of Protestant reform at home and abroad; and he was a famous soldier who died in battle for the cause of Protestantism. Sydney was England's greatest "Rennaissance man," whose broad interests, far reaching education, religious fervor and fierce patriotism make him a good example of the worldview of this period.

More specifically, characteristics of a Renaissance world view include the following details:

- Interest in classical (that is, Greek and Roman) learning and in the original versions of ancient texts, including those of the Old and New Testaments;
- Interest in the *studia humanitatis* (literally, the "study of things human"): language, literature, history, art and government. These subjects were seen as distinct from the medieval disciplines of theology, philosophy and law, which concerned God rather than man. The Renaissance emphasis on these subjects is the origin of the terms *humanism* and the *humanities*. It is quite distinct from (and not to be confused with) *secular humanism*, a 20th century social and political philosophy.
- Interest in the issue of true religion and how it should be realized in the world. This was the question of the Protestant Reformation and it had literary as well as political implications both in England and in her American colonies.
- Interest in human government and how it should be structured. This issue surfaced in a variety of Renaissance era works, from the treatises of Hobbes and Locke to the plays of Shakespeare and the sermons of the Massachusetts Bay Puritans.

Authors: Renaissance Literature

Poets
Sir Thomas Wyatt (1503-1542)
Sir Walter Raleigh (1552-1618)
John Donne (1572-1631)
George Herbert (1593-1633)
Andrew Marvell (1621-1678)

Sir Thomas More (1478-1535)
Utopia (1516)

Edmund Spenser (1552-1599)
The Shepheardes Calender (1579)
The Faerie Queene (1590, 1596)

Sir Philip Sydney (1554-1586)
Arcadia (1590)
Astrophil and Stella (1591)

William Shakespeare (1564-1616)
Hamlet (c. 1599)
Much Ado About Nothing (c. 1598)
Henry V (c. 1599)
Poems

Christopher Marlowe (1564-1593)
Dr. Faustus (1592)

Ben Jonson (1572-1637)
Volpone (1606)
The Alchemist (1610)
Poems

Thomas Hobbes (1588-1679)
Leviathan (1651)

John Winthrop (1588-1649)
A Model of Christian Charity (1630)

William Bradford (1590-1657)
Of Plymouth Plantation (written 1630-1647; first published 1856)

Roger Williams (1603-1683)
The Bloody Tenet of Persecution for the Cause of Conscience (1644)

John Milton (1608-1674)
Lycidas (1637)
Paradise Lost (1667)
Samson Agonistes (1671)

Anne Bradstreet (1612-1672)
The Tenth Muse Lately Sprung up in America (1650) – the first American poetry ever published

John Bunyan (1628-1688)
The Pilgrim's Progress (1675) – a Renaissance work, though written in the neo-classical period

Other Works of Renaissance Literature:

_____

_____

_____

_____

_____

_____

_____

_____

_____

_____

_____

_____

_____

_____

_____

_____

_____

_____

_____

_____

III. Neo-classical Literature (1660 – 1800)

Some have described the period after the restoration of Charles II as "a new age of elegance" in literature. Reacting against the intricacy, flamboyance, boldness and extravagance of the late Renaissance, writers in this period tended to favor simplicity, clarity, restraint, regularity and good sense. They were interested in discovering the rules that govern the world and then working within them to produce beauty – in fact, the rules themselves often became the subject of their work, which is part of the reason for the interest in literary criticism and political theory throughout this period.

The neo-classical period gets its name from the fact that these writers often strove to imitate the style of ancient Roman authors like Virgil, Ovid and Horace, who wrote during the reign of Augustus Caesar in the first century AD. Neo-classical writers were also sensitive to the issues of their own day, however, and it is instructive to notice that this period in literature coincided with the development of rationalistic philosophies, the rise of experimental science and a general desire for peace and order after an era of violent religious and political extremism.

Some ideas common to many writers during the neo-classical period include:

- A negative view of the natural passions. Neo-classical authors assumed that natural passions should be subordinated to social needs and strictly controlled. The writings of Benjamin Franklin on this subject are perfectly illustrative of the neo-classical worldview. Hobbes' *Leviathan* is a good example of a Renaissance era work that foreshadowed the neo-classical period in this respect.

- A positive view of natural human reason. Perhaps because experimental science was gaining popularity, neo-classical authors began to assume that man's methodical use of his rational powers could lead him to truth in a variety of areas, whether philosophical, political or religious. Even preachers in this period demonstrated this way of thinking, as the writings of the American Jonathan Edwards illustrate.

- A search for meaning in the order of things. Neoclassical thinkers believed order – in nature, social hierarchies, government and religion – was the source of happiness and contentment. Even the order within literary forms was an end in and of itself.

- A concern for the needs of society before the needs of the individual. This idea helps explain why you see lots of constitutions and political theory in the neoclassical period, and why authors such as John Locke were so influential.

An important note: American writers of this period, while sharing many of the philosophical concerns and stylistic tendencies of their English counterparts, were nevertheless engaged in a separate set of intellectual struggles brought on by the unique demands of their New World society. This struggle gave rise to the development of a unique literature which we call Colonial American. It is included here with that designation.

Authors: Neo-classical literature in England

John Locke (1632-1704)
Essay Concerning Human Understanding (1690)
Two Treatises of Government (1690)

John Dryden (1637-1700)
Absalom and Achitophel (1681)
Translation of Virgil (1697)
Poems

Daniel Defoe (1660-1731)
Robinson Crusoe (1719)

Jonathan Swift (1667-1745)
Gulliver's Travels (1726)

Alexander Pope (1688-1744)
The Rape of the Lock (1712)
Poems

Samuel Johnson (1709-1784)
Translation of Horace (1784)
Dictionary (1755)
Lives of the Poets (1781)
Poems

Authors: Colonial American Literature

Cotton Mather (1663-1728)
Magnalia Christi Americana (1702)

Mary Rowlandson (c. 1637-c.1711)
Captivity Narrative (1682)

Edward Taylor (1642-1729)
Poems

Jonathan Edwards (1703-1758)
Personal Narrative (c. 1740)
Sinners in the Hands of an Angry God (1741)

Benjamin Franklin (1706-1790)
Autobiography (1771-1790, published 1791)
Poor Richard's Almanac (1732-1757)

J. Hector St. John de Crevecoeur (1735-1813)
Letters from an American Farmer (1782)

Thomas Paine (1737-1809)
 Common Sense (1776)
 The American Crisis (1776)
 The Age of Reason (1793)

Thomas Jefferson (1743-1826)
 Declaration of Independence (1776)
 Notes on the State of Virginia (1785)

Other Works of Neo-classical and Colonial American Literature:

_____

_____

_____

_____

_____

_____

_____

_____

_____

_____

_____

_____

_____

_____

_____

_____

_____

_____

_____

_____

IV. Romantic Literature (1800 – 1865)

Romanticism as a literary movement arose in the late 18th century during in the aftermath of the French Revolution. In many ways, Romanticism was a reaction against the formal, orderly literature of the neo-classical period. Its beginning is commonly associated with the publication of William Wordsworth's *Lyrical Ballads* in 1798. In England, the Romantic period ended in 1832 with the death of Sir Walter Scott, one of its most famous novelists. In America, however, the Romantic impulse continued through the Civil War – Harriet Beecher Stowe and Abraham Lincoln were both affected by Romanticism, as were many of the preachers and politicians of the antebellum period.

Romanticism is no easier to define than any other literary movement, but Romantics tended to share certain general assumptions about the world, including faith in mankind's innate goodness and eventual perfectibility. They saw men as equal at birth, individually unique and capable of infinite self-development. They stressed the value of expressing human abilities that were common to all from birth rather than from training. Romantics owed a debt to French philosopher Jean Jacques Rousseau, whose image of the noble savage became their ideal vision of humanity freed from the stifling boundaries of civilization.

Romantics in England were poets more often than not, although novelists such as Scott and Jane Austen also belong to the period. The works of Romantic authors are likely to deal with themes such as the following:

Radical individualism

Neo-classical literature had described men and women as limited beings in a strictly ordered world which changed little from generation to generation. The limits of the human species were often the subjects, not only of fiction but also of philosophy and political theory. The glory of neo-classical literature was to exult in order, precedent, long-established principles and common sense.

Romantic authors reacted strongly against this tradition, and put immense faith in the power and potential of the individual man. The individual who refuses to submit to limitations (whether of species, class, race or sex) is often the hero in Romantic fiction, because he is the true human being. Earlier ages might have called this striving sin; the Romantics called it a triumph.

Romantic works often depict characters isolated from society or at least struggling against its rules and regulations: Cain, Satan, Faust, Prometheus, Napoleon, the Ancient Mariner and Hester Prynne are good examples.

Nature

The description of scenery and natural imagery figured prominently in many works of the Romantic period. Nature was often used as a symbol of the freedom of the human soul when unfettered by the restraints imposed by society. Scenic beauty reminded Romantic authors of the possibilities of the human soul, and they used Nature as a model for harmony in the world. If we could all act according to our pure, essential natures, they argued, we would get along much better.

Romantic works therefore tend to advocate the emotional, intuitive and sensual side of the human experience against the orderly, restrained demands of established human society. Hawthorne's *The Scarlet Letter* is a wonderful example of this theme in action, complete with symbolism and imagery that perfectly illustrate the Romantic faith in Nature. The novels of James Fenimore Cooper also show these assumptions very clearly.

Imagination

Among Romanticism's most characteristic traits was faith in the individual imagination and its ability to triumph over the senses. Romantic authors believed that the chief aim of life was learning to "see" the world through the imagination, and so transcend its troubles and difficulties. The Romantics saw a supernatural power in the individual imagination – a power strong enough literally to remake the world. By demonstrating this imagination at work in their poems and novels, they hoped to effect a revolution just as real as the ones the French and Americans had attempted in the late 18th century. The essays of Ralph Waldo Emerson, though not fiction, are important in this regard, as are the poems of William Wordsworth, Samuel Taylor Coleridge and Lord Byron.

Authors: English Romanticism

Poets

William Worsdworth (1770-1850)
Samuel Taylor Coleridge (1772-1834)
George Gordon, Lord Byron (1788-1824)
Percy Bysshe Shelley (1792-1822)
John Keats (1795-1821)

Sir Walter Scott (1771-1832)

Rob Roy (1817)
The Heart of Midlothian (1818)
Ivanhoe (1819)

Jane Austen (1775-1817)

Sense and Sensibility (1811)
Pride and Prejudice (1813)
Emma (1815)
Persuasion (1817)

Mary Shelley (1797-1851)

Frankenstein (1818) – this novel belongs to a subcategory of Romantic fiction, the Gothic terror novel.

Authors: American Romanticism

Washington Irving (1783-1859)

History of New York (1809)
Sketchbook of Geoffrey Crayon (1820) – contains "Rip van Winkle" and "The Legend of Sleepy Hollow"

Tales of a Traveler (1824)

James Fenimore Cooper (1789-1851)
The Pioneers (1823)
Last of the Mohicans (1826)
The Prairie (1827)
The Pathfinder (1840)
The Deerslayer (1841)

Ralph Waldo Emerson (1803-1882)
Nature (1836)
Concord Hymn (1837)
Self-Reliance (1841)
The Over-Soul (1841)
Poems

Nathaniel Hawthorne (1804-1864)
The Scarlet Letter (1850)
The House of Seven Gables (1851)
The Blithedale Romance (1852)

Henry Wadsworth Longfellow (1807-1882)
Poems on Slavery (1842)
Evangeline (1847)
The Song of Hiawatha (1855)
Tales of a Wayside Inn (1863), includes "Paul Revere's Ride"

Edgar Allan Poe (1809-1849) – like Mary Shelley, a Gothic terror writer
The Fall of the House of Usher (1839)
The Murders in the Rue Morgue (1841)
The Raven (1845)
A Descent into the Maelstrom (1845)
The Cask of Amontillado (1846)
Annabel Lee (1849)
The Masque of the Red Death (1850)
The Telltale Heart (1850)
The Pit and the Pendulum (1850)

Henry David Thoreau (1817-1862)
Civil Disobedience (1849)
Walden (1854)

Herman Melville (1819-1891)
Moby Dick (1851)
Billy Budd, Sailor (first published in 1924)

Harriet Beecher Stowe (1811-1896)
Uncle Tom's Cabin (1852)

Other Works of Romantic Literature:

_____

_____

_____

_____

_____

_____

_____

_____

_____

_____

_____

_____

_____

_____

_____

_____

_____

_____

_____

V. Realist Literature (1840-1900)

The beginning of the reign of Queen Victoria (1837) is usually considered the dawn of literary Realism. This period lasted throughout the 19th century in England and well into the 20th century in America. Just as Romanticism had been a reaction against Neo-classicism, Realism was a reaction against Romanticism. Where Romantics stressed the limitless potential of the individual imagination, Realists preferred a faithful representation of the facts. It has been said that Romantics saw the individual as a god, while Realists saw him as a common man. In any event, Realists were less concerned with human potential than with human problems.

Where Romantics looked to an ideal world free from the corruption of civilization, Realists concerned themselves with the world as it was. Their works were thus characterized by attention to the social, economic and political issues of the 19th century. These included the problems of industrialization and urbanization, as in Charles Dickens' novels about London's lower classes; the relationship between traditional religion and new philosophies such as Darwinism, as in Rudyard Kipling's descriptions of Imperial India; and the problems of poverty and inequality, as in Mark Twain's treatment of American slavery.

Where Romantics had encouraged readers to see "through" their eyes to an idealized reality beyond the senses, Realists preferred to see "with" their eyes what was actually before them. Above all, realist fiction emphasized the accurate representation of detail. A wonderful (and hilarious) example of the difference between Realism and Romanticism on this point is Mark Twain's essay entitled "James Fenimore Cooper's Literary Offenses," in which Twain evaluates the Romantic use of description from a Realist's perspective.

In England, the Realist movement took place during the reign of Queen Victoria (r. 1837-1901), and so it is known as the Victorian period.

Authors: Victorian Literature

Thomas Carlyle (1795-1881)
Sartor Resartus (1833-1834)
The French Revolution (1837)
The Life of John Sterling (1851)

Charles Dickens (1812-1870)
The Pickwick Papers (1836-1837)
The Adventures of Oliver Twist (1837-1839)
The Life and Adventures of Nicholas Nickleby (1838-1839)
Barnaby Rudge (1841)
A Christmas Carol (1843)
David Copperfield (1849-1850)
Bleak House (1852-1853)
A Tale of Two Cities (1859)
Great Expectations (1860-1861)

William Makepeace Thackeray (1811-1863)
Vanity Fair (1848)

George Eliot (1819-1880)
Adam Bede (1859)
Silas Marner (1861)
Middlemarch (1871-1872)

Emily Bronte (1818-1848)
Wuthering Heights (1847)

Charlotte Bronte (1816-1855)
Jane Eyre (1847)

Thomas Hardy (1840-1928)
Jude the Obscure (1895)

Rudyard Kipling (1865-1936)
Gunga Din (1890)
The Jungle Book (1894)
The Second Jungle Book (1895)
Captains Courageous (1897)
Kim (1901)

Authors: American Realism

Mark Twain (1835-1910)
The Celebrated Jumping Frog of Calaveras County (1867)
The Innocents Abroad (1869)
The Adventures of Tom Sawyer (1876)
The Prince and the Pauper (1882)
The Adventures of Huckleberry Finn (1884)
A Connecticut Yankee in King Arthur's Court (1889)
Fenimore Cooper's Literary Offenses (1895)
The Man that Corrupted Hadleyburg (1900)

William Dean Howells (1837-1920)
A Chance Acquaintance (1873)
A Modern Insurance (1882)
The Rise of Silas Lapham (1884)
Indian Summer (1885)
The Kentons (1902)

Henry James (1843-1916)
The Portrait of a Lady (1881)
The Wings of the Dove (1902)
The Ambassadors (1903)
The Golden Bowl (1904)

Kate Chopin (1850-1904)
*The Awakening (1889) – this novel exhibits a Romantic prose style
even though it was written during the age of Realism.*

Naturalism

Naturalism may be considered a distinct form of realism that lasted until the First World War. Naturalism was an extension of realism, in the sense that naturalist authors were also concerned about the real world. They focused on this world for slightly different reasons, however: many naturalists were adherents of Darwin's theory of evolution and denied the existence of anything beyond the physical senses.

Naturalists believed that man's existence is determined entirely by blind external or biological forces such as heredity and the environment. Since most naturalist authors were atheists, their works also tended to stress the role of chance rather than Providence or Fate in determining life's outcomes. If Romantics saw the individual as a god and Realists saw him as a common man, Naturalists saw him as a helpless animal.

Naturalists often wrote about the fringes of society – the criminal, the fallen and the down-and-out – in order to draw attention to the animalistic nature of man. In many naturalist works, man shares characteristics with the animal world, and is not much better off than brute beasts when it comes to controlling his environment or his destiny.

Authors: Naturalism

Edith Wharton (1862-1937)
The House of Mirth (1905)
Ethan Frome (1912)
The Age of Innocence (1920)

Frank Norris (1870-1902)
McTeague (1899)
The Octopus (1901)
The Pit (1903)

Stephen Crane (1871-1900)
Red Badge of Courage (1895)

Theodore Dreiser (1871-1945)
Sister Carrie (1900)

Jack London (1876-1916)
To Build a Fire (1902)
The Call of the Wild (1903)
The Sea Wolf (1904)
White Fang (1906)

Other Works of Realist Literature:

_____

_____

_____

_____

_____

_____

_____

_____

_____

_____

_____

_____

_____

_____

_____

_____

_____

_____

_____

_____

_____

_____

VI. Modernist Literature (1900-1945)

The Modern period in English language literature dawned in the early 20th century as Western civilization began to undergo cataclysmic changes. These changes caused widespread feelings of disorientation, rootlessness and uncertainty. Writers of the modern period were motivated by the sense that an old world had passed away and there was nothing with which to replace it.

The ideas of Karl Marx undermined faith in 19th century models for economic and political progress. World War I had destroyed that century's geopolitical system and offered no guarantees of future stability. Dramatic innovations in technology became widely available, including telephones, radios, phonographs, moving pictures and automobiles. By making communication and transportation easier, these inventions fostered restlessness and dissatisfaction. The growth of modern science, embodied in Einstein's theory of Relativity and Darwin's theory of evolution, undermined faith in the traditional Christian explanations of natural phenomena. The social ideas of Sigmund Freud led to unsettling conclusions about traditional family relationships. Political controversies surrounding prohibition and women's suffrage added to the feeling that the whole world was turning upside down.

Modernist literature attempted to convey this sense of uncertainty and to depict a society in decay. Where the Realists of the late 19th century still held to the idea that society was something stable that could be accurately described, modernists felt forced by the events of their time to reject this assumption. At the heart of modernist literature was the conviction that the traditional structures of human life – religious, social, political, economic and artistic – had either been destroyed or proven false.

Modernist fiction reflected this conviction in its style and structure. The typical modernist story comes across as a collection of disjointed fragments. It will seem to begin arbitrarily, to advance without explanation and to end without resolution, consisting of vivid segments juxtaposed without cushioning or integrating transitions. For this reason, modernist stories such as Hemingway's *The Sun Also Rises* can be unsettling to the reader.

Modernist works are often spare of language, compressed, vivid and direct. They often portray characters who exhibit none of the traits that earlier ages would have ascribed to heroes. The protagonists in a modernist story are often aimless and defeated, frustrated in their search for meaning.

Authors: Modernism

Willa Cather (1873-1947)
O Pioneers! (1913)
My Antonia (1918)
Death comes for the Archbishop (1927)

James Joyce (1882-1941)
A Portrait of the Artist as a Young Man (1916)

Ulysses (1922)
Finnegan's Wake (1939)

Virginia Woolf (1882-1941
Mrs. Dalloway (1925)
To the Lighthouse (1927)
Orlando (1928)

T.S. Eliot (1888-1965)
The Love Song of J. Alfred Prufrock (1917)
The Waste Land (1922)
The Hollow Men (1925)
Ash Wednesday (1930)

F. Scott Fitzgerald (1896-1940)
The Beautiful and the Damned (1922)
This Side of Paradise (1920)
The Great Gatsby (1925)
Tender is the Night (1934)

William Faulkner (1897-1962)
The Sound and the Fury (1929)
As I Lay Dying (1930)
Light in August (1932)
Absalom, Absalom! (1936)
The Unvanquished (1938)

Ernest Hemingway (1899-1961)
The Sun Also Rises (1926)
A Farewell to Arms (1929)
Winner Take Nothing (1933)
The Snows of Kilamanjaro (1936)
To Have and Have Not (1937)
For Whom the Bell Tolls (1940)
The Old Man and the Sea (1952)

John Steinbeck (1902-1968)
Of Mice and Men (1937)
The Grapes of Wrath (1939)
The Pearl (1947)
East of Eden (1952)

Other Works of Modernist Literature:

A Warning Against "Christian Deconstruction"
By Missy Andrews

There is, in the Christian homeschool community, a troublesome interpretive error that has, to my knowledge, gone unaddressed. That problem, for lack of better words, I will call Christian Deconstruction. Most errors are, by nature, unintentional. I hope that a brief discussion of the history and methods of literary analytical principles will arm Christian thinkers and readers against this particular error and encourage both sound reading and good scholarship. While a discussion of this sort will by nature tend towards the abstract and philosophical, it is good to remember that ideas have consequences, and that the consequences of error, even unintentional errors, have over the course of history often proven to be disastrous.

Literary deconstruction is a way of reading. Readers who employ this method believe an author's words outstrip his intentions. In truth, for the literary deconstructionist, the original intentions of an author matter very little. Jacques Derrida, the father of Literary Deconstruction, describes in his Grammatology what he believes to be the impossibility of finding any straightforward meaning in printed matter. Starting from philosophical atheism, Derrida reasons that apart from an objective reference point that stands outside of creation, all things become relative to the individual. His idea that language itself, therefore, cannot bear any objective meaning follows logically. In the absence of any objective meaning, Derrida suggests the job of the literary analyst is to take apart the meaning of a text (literally to deconstruct it) rather than to discover meaning within it. As the reader infuses meaning into other authors' written words, he participates in the creative process and supplies a unique interpretation of the original work. By this manner of thinking, textual meaning is divorced from the original intentions of the author and dependent upon the creativity of the reader. By virtue of Derrida's interpretive methodology, all interpretations of this sort must be considered equally valid and may be distinguished one from another not by their general accuracy or truth to the text, but by virtue of creativity and, sometimes (more's the pity) titillation.

Christian literary analysis requires less creativity and more scholarship. Literary analysis worthy of the name is the process of reading carefully in attempt to hear the voice of an author, the real creative force behind a work. This requires great humility and self-control of the reader. It asks the reader to lay aside his own preconceived notions, personal thoughts, and ideas in order to hear those of another. Good readers are good listeners. The first job of a student is to read closely to discover the innate meaning of an author's purposefully chosen words.

Reading is not primarily a quest for self-discovery. It is an encounter with "others" – other people, other cultures, others' thoughts, others' feelings, others' experiences. It is true that such encounters often stimulate responses as we attempt first to understand, and then to identify with authors. Creative thought produces more creative thought. This, however, is merely a beautiful by-product of reading, rather than its primary object. First, we read to understand.

Reading of this kind presupposes a static text. That is to say, the reader must recognize that the work before him is complete. It will not in any way morph or change to communicate anything beyond the scope and intentions of its author. It says what it says. Meaning is authorial intention. The goal of a good reader is to discover what the author meant by what he wrote, that is – to understand him.

This kind of reading considers a work in its context, that is, in relationship both to its place and time in history and in the body of its author's work. This kind of reading considers or receives the work as an organic whole, fully developed and artistically complete. Good readers recognize that the literature they study is intelligently crafted. They look to understand the design of a piece by closely examining the work's structure and stylistic emphases. They do this in attempt to discover the underlying questions or conflicts that provoked the author's art, and to hear his proposed solutions and thoughts on the matter.

Good readers must consider the meaning of individual words based both on their contextual use within a specific piece, and in their historical sense. They must study the history of a document, not only to understand the era from which it emerged, but also the concerns of the man who wrote it. What was his background? What was his understanding of the world and its significance? What were the great issues of his society? All of these questions contribute to an honest reading of a piece of literature.

Truly, it is this kind of reading that makes the study of literature so beneficial. For by it, a student can learn to thoughtfully consider the ideas of others. He will inevitably encounter a great variety of personalities and worldviews. He may, in his reading, encounter a militant communist or a naturalist atheist. He may converse with a postmodernist, developing empathy for the man while discerning the danger of his ideas. He may listen to the ideas of any number of thinkers - hear them articulate their thoughts, their passions and concerns in their own voice. He may, from the safety of his living room, view the lay of the land, philosophically speaking - see the intellectual landscape, the pinnacles of Truth and the dark valleys of error that give way, road by road, to his own intellectual locale. In this way, he may become more aware of himself and his world. He may, in this way, learn to discriminate between philosophies, see the discrepancies between them, separate truth from error, think critically.

Literary Deconstruction robs readers of all of this. It encourages sloppy scholarship, narcissism and arrogance. It erodes good thinking. It produces bad readers.

Deconstruction has produced many "creative" interpretations of literature. Go to any college library and find a multitude of these: feminist interpretations, Freudian interpretations, racial interpretations. These "special" interpretations abound. Having cut the umbilical cord of the text from its authorial parent, the textual progeny is left to become whatever its reader will make of it.

The Literary Deconstructionists' ambition in reading is not to understand the author's thoughts, but to probe and air their own. For Deconstructionists, what really matters is self-expression and personal creativity. Analysts of this stripe teach students to ask, "What does the story mean to me?" In pursuit of themselves, they press every text into their own image, manipulating language to serve their own agendas. C.S. Lewis, in his Experiment In Criticism, says readers like these meet only themselves in the books they read. Such readers are pitiable. For, having been bequeathed the wealth of their ancestors' wisdom, they, blind fools, choose to remain in the relative poverty of their own narrow experience.

Many of you might be wondering what all of this has to do with you. Unfortunately, the Freudian, feminist, and racial literary analysts are not alone in their blindness. I write because of the startling number of Christian readers I have met who likewise seek a "Christian interpretation" of books. With the best of intentions, these Christian Deconstructionists commit the same error as their liberal counterparts. They utilize the same analytical methodologies as the special interest groups, separating texts from authors and manipulating them to fit their own philosophical agenda. In the process, they do the same violence to texts and their authors as their atheistic counterparts. In truth, there is no "Christian interpretation" of a work of literature, any more than there is a feminist interpretation or a Freudian interpretation or an African-American interpretation. The only honest critical interpretation is a scholarly one, historically accurate and contextually consistent.

We created our worldview seminar as an extension of our Teaching the Classics basic seminar. Our intention was to build upon the foundational principle of careful reading by teaching some further questions to ask of stories in order to determine the general worldview of an author as it is expressed within the pages of the text. Our goal was to encourage a comparative study of worldview and philosophy through literature. Many participants, however, attend the seminar in the hope of discovering how to apply their own Christian worldview to the books they read. They wish in this way to baptize the literature they encounter and rid it of its defects, to sanitize it for their children.

Many Christian parents fear that exposing their children to the ideas of non-Christians will corrupt them. They are motivated by concern that their children will be harmed by the faulty worldviews of the authors they read. Some of these worldviews are worth fearing – communistic atheism, post-modernism, naturalism in its various garbs. All good parents want to protect their children's minds and hearts from these. Unfortunately, misreading the stories that express these worldviews is not the answer. It is not only inherently dishonest, but it also reduces the potential of the literature to instruct and enlighten the student.

What does it mean to read like Christians? Is there such a thing as a Christian Literary Criticism? The Bible encourages believers to be humble, kind, charitable people, slow to speak and quick to hear (James 1:19). With this exhortation in mind, perhaps reading "Christianly" means nothing more than applying oneself to understand the words of an author, striving to "hear" him. A Christian's first principle of literary analysis ought to be to tell the truth.

This means reading Jack London and finding within his work not statements about Jehovah God and His ways, but statements about Mother Nature and hers. This is because Jack London's work expresses Literary Naturalism, a philosophy grounded in atheistic determinism. His stories express and explore the philosophy of evolution. In London's works, impersonal nature takes the place of God. In the light of this atheistic materialism, London's world reads doubly cold.

Why should Christians read stories rooted in such faulty philosophies? Do they not threaten the worldview of Christian readers? In order to answer these questions, it is important to remember two things. First, reading about an idea doesn't make it yours. Second, the Truth is the greatest defense against lies. Making students aware of the fact that writers write to communicate ideas, and making clear to them that all ideas are not good ideas protects them from being unwittingly influenced by the books they read. Furthermore, by discussing the ideas occurring in books, students and parents are able to flesh out the presuppositions upon which such ideas are based. Parents then have the priceless opportunity of holding up those presuppositions to the light of the gospel, helping their students to compare the premises of each. In this way, the errors of faulty worldviews are exposed by the light of the Gospel, and the student's faith, far from being sabotaged by offensive doctrine, is shored up by it.

Understanding London's naturalism and evolutionary sentiments doesn't make the reader a naturalist and evolutionist. On the contrary, London, with cold clarity, portrays his skewed worldview to be as unfriendly and inhospitable as the arctic conditions in which his story is set. Moreover, by hearing such worldviews articulated by the voices of their historical advocates, the worldviews are condemned, so to speak, by their own proponents. Christian parents need not condemn London's philosophies. London's characterization of them is condemnation enough. London's views cannot and should not be baptized. They cannot be Christianized. What fellowship has light with darkness? The best that can be done is to allow the stark perversity of London's atheistic pragmatism to speak for itself - to allow chiaroscuro (light and shadow) to have its effect.

Christian parents need have no fear of good reading. Rather than posing a threat to their children, careful reading protects them. Critical reading trains a student to listen with the intent of understanding people who may not be like them. What is more, if an author has consistently and truthfully represented his ideas and questions within the context of his worldview, the student will inevitably find pathos in his work that demands compassion.

The classics have withstood time because they ask enduring, universal questions. Having encountered these, students will have better chance of avoiding the arrogance that comes all too often to those who have been given answers to questions they have never asked. In this way, these good readers will be better ambassadors for Christ in a perishing populace. They will become compassionate participants in the Great Conversation. Good listeners become good communicators.

Christian parents and literary analysts have great opportunity to weigh in with truth in the marketplace of ideas. However, good conversations are not monologues. Therefore, it is incumbent upon readers to avoid the impulse to turn every written document into a statement of their own worldview. Let us listen to the ideas of others. Let us strive to understand them fully. Let us consider the questions they pose and the struggles they face. And let us, with humility, scholarship, and integrity, extend to the people that hold these ideas the hope that Christ has extended to us – that in the midst of vain philosophies, false hopes, and fallen mankind there exists grace, goodness, and a pervasive beauty that will inevitably transform all things into the likeness of Christ.

A Summary of Some Prevalent Worldviews

Every worldview has at its foundation two important questions, asked by all thinking men since the dawn of history: *Who is God?* and *What is Man?* Since good literature deals with humanity's universal questions, you can expect to find some version of these questions at the heart of any author's meditations. A man's assumptions about himself and his God influence everything he thinks, regardless of the subject. Of course, there are multiple ways to answer the questions.

Answers to the question: Who is God?

The two simplest answers to the question *Who is God?* are found in the responses of Theism and Atheism. Theists acknowledge the existence of God, although their understanding of Who He is varies. Atheists deny the existence of any supernatural being. Some refuse to answer the question based on what they believe is insufficient information. This plea of uncertainty is referred to as agnosticism. In order to simplify our discussion of Worldview, we'll begin by categorizing the various major worldviews as either theistic or atheistic:

Theistic

> *Christianity*
> *Deism*
> *Judaism*
> *Islam*
> *Cosmic Humanism*

Atheistic

> *Marxist-Leninism*
> *Secular Humanism*
> *Modernism*
> *Postmodernism*
> *Environmentalism*

Notice that the category " Theism" merely acknowledges the existence of God. It doesn't indicate the kind of god in question. In order to further understand worldviews, it is necessary to ask what kind of supernatural being the worldview acknowledges. For example:

Is the supernatural being singular (monotheism) or plural (polytheism)?

Monotheistic Worldviews

Christianity
Deism
Judaism
Islam

Polytheistic Worldviews

Cosmic Humanism

Is the god personal or impersonal in nature?

Worldviews that acknowledge a personal god, who both exhibits a distinct personality and interacts individually with man, include:

Christianity
Judaism
Islam

Is the god separate from man and nature or a part of man and nature?

In addition, it is necessary to distinguish whether the god is distinct from man and creation or a part of man and creation.

God is distinct from man and creation

Deism
Christianity
Judaism
Islam

God is one with man and creation

Cosmic Humanism
Pantheism

It is easy to see that the more questions one asks, the clearer the divisions between worldviews become.

What of the second foundational question for worldview study, *What is Man?* An individual may answer this question in a variety of ways. He might say man is a collection of electrically animated cells and matter. He might say man is a creature made in the image of God. He may say he is the most highly evolved animal in nature. He may say he is perfectible. He may say he is fatally flawed by sin. Even this brief list of possible answers reveals the significance of the question. If man is merely cells and matter, he is no more than a part of creation itself, and as such, warrants no special privilege compared to other organisms. If he is the most evolved, then he has gained the right through intellect and luck to leverage his position in nature. If he is mostly good and finally perfectible, then he is not to be feared. If he is fatally flawed by sin, he is to be regarded with suspicion.

Answers to these questions produce consequences in the practical life of the thinker, as well as in the lives of those with whom he interacts. This is why worldview thinking is so important.

A brief definition of the dominant worldviews may aid the student of Worldview Analysis:

Theistic Worldviews

Christianity – Monotheistic in nature, Christianity testifies to a triune God who manifested Himself personally to man in the historic, loving person of Jesus Christ, the image of God incarnate. Christian doctrine teaches that man was made in the image of God. Christians therefore regard man as the pinnacle of God's creation, thought hey acknowledge that he is fatally flawed by sin. This doctrine explains why men demonstrate both good and evil behaviors. Christians believe that the incarnate God, Jesus, sought man out and died to pay the penalty for man's sin, rising again from the dead because He was stronger than death. He promises relationship with God for those who put their faith in Him. Christians relate to their God on the basis of His work for them.

Deism – Deism, too, is monotheistic in nature. However, Deists deny the personal nature of God. Although they consider God the source of all things, they see him as a watchmaker who created the watch that is the world, wound it up and walked away. Although this God is powerful and creative, He is disinterested in the world He made and in man.

Judaism – Also monotheistic in nature, Judaism appeals to the commands of the Torah: "Hear, O Israel, the Lord thy God is One God." Jews acknowledge the justice and mercy of this creator God who established personal relationship with the nation of Israel, and they continue to await the Messiah, the Deliverer He promised through the words of His prophets. They believe this Messiah will rescue them from their sin and apostasy. The source of their doctrine and faith is the Old Testament, which they regard as holy scripture. Jews relate to their god on the basis of their works and His mercy.

Islam – Islam, too, is monotheistic in nature. Followers of Islam are called Muslims, and they call their god Allah. Muslim believers regard the first five books of the Old Testament as holy writ, together with the writings of Mohammed, the first prophet of Islam. However, they maintain that their holy book, the Quran, alone is uncorrupted. Muslims appeal to the Quran, together with the Hadith, the book of Muslim teachings, traditions, rulings and the actions of Mohammed and his cohorts, for their belief system. They believe that man is perfectible through obedience to divinely given laws they call pillars of Islam. Paradise awaits those who obey Allah, just as Hell awaits the disobedient. Muslims relate to Allah on the basis of their works.

Cosmic Humanism – Cosmic Humanists believe that "everything is God and that God is everything." Consequently, Cosmic Humanists affirm their own deity, the deity of those around them, and even the deity of the natural world (a concept called *pantheism*). They encourage all people to acknowledge their divine consciousness. Because Cosmic Humanists believe in the eternal nature of the soul (gods, after all, cannot die), they affirm the rebirth of the soul through reincarnation.

Atheistic Worldviews

Marxist-Leninism –This worldview is named for its most important proponents, Karl Marx and Vladimir Lenin. Marxist-Leninists (also called Communists) deny the existence of God and hold a naturalistic view of the world. Naturalists believe in only the things they can see, touch, taste, smell or hear. Because of this, naturalists are sometimes referred to as materialists. Most Marxist-Leninists acknowledge Darwin's theory of evolution, as well as the concept of survival of the fittest. They believe that man is primarily good, but corrupted by greed which evidences itself in the form of social classes. Their goal is to create a utopia on earth in the form of a classless society. In order to effect this, they propose a communist ecomomy, sanctioned and maintained by the state. Since they reject the existence of God, they appeal to positive law in which the state determines all law and morality. Communists consider religion oppressive and counterproductive and aim to eradicate it through both law and force.

Secular Humanism – Secular Humanists reject the existence of God. As atheists, they acknowledge man alone as the source of intelligent thought and action. They affirm Darwin's theory of evolution. Consequently, they appeal to man, the most evolved species in nature, for the solution to all of earth's problems. Science and reason are preferred in man's quest to master nature. Here, too, morality is determined by appeal to power-brokers.

Modernism – Modernism refers to an intellectual period which began in the late 19th century and continued into the 20th century. Thinkers in this period faced the growing mechanisation of a rising industrial society and the impersonal nature of city living. Populations were shifting from rural to urban areas. Families, which had historically cohered for the purpose of agrarian productivity, scattered. Enlightenment thinking had unseated theology and crowned physical science as the queen of the sciences, declaring the existence of God unnecessary to explain the physical world. Two world wars evoked a growing pessimism in this fragmented society. In a world without footholds, modernists rejected traditional ideas of truth, goodness, and beauty, embracing nihilism instead. Without the morality previous generations gleaned from a stable, religious ideal, modernists felt forced to create their own ethic.

Postmodernism – Perhaps the most consistent atheistic thought system is Postmodernism. Postmodernists reject all absolutes. Because even atheism makes the absolute statement that there is no god, some Postmodernists prefer agnosticism. Founders of Postmodernist thought include Jacques Derrida and Michel Foucault. Derrida, in particular, created an interpretive device he called deconstruction. Predicated on the assumption that there is no ultimate reality, Derrida maintained that words themselves, which purport to reference reality, are essentially pliable and void of any static meaning. It is for the reader to supply words with meaning, and he must do so independently of the author who wrote them. Thus, the reader deconstructs the original author's meaning to create his own. Ultimately, Derrida's philosophy suggests that verbal communication is essentially impossible. Postmodernists embrace this critical theory and build from it a social pluralism. Each man, the postmodernist would say, creates his own meaning. Therefore, there is no ultimate Truth or morality, only small truths local social groups agree upon. Once again, the state is acknowledged as the source of law and ethics (positive law). However, one society's moral good may very well be perceived as another society's moral evil. Religion is perceived not as the source of overarching Truth, but rather as the expression of personal preference. Postmodernism embraces pluralism and tolerance.

Environmentalism – Environmentalism begins with the premise that the material world is all man can know. Since earth outlives man, man is beholden to acknowledge earth's superiority. Earth is, in a sense, god. Man trespasses for a lifetime on the planet; his job is to leave no footprint. This contradicts the Christian teaching of the dominion mandate which encourages man to develop and utilize earth's resources as faithful steward of a world designed to house him and his posterity.

For more information about

CenterForLit products and programs,

contact us at

(509) 738-2837

adam@centerforlit.com

missy@centerforlit.com

or visit us on the web at

www.centerforlit.com